1ST GRADE PHONICS
Unit 6
Spelling Long Vowels

TABLE OF CONTENTS

IMPORTANT: Please refer to the Teacher Guide for specific scripts, procedures, and words that are represented by pictures.

Throughout this Unit, learners will scan QR codes. Be careful they scan each code individually.

LEARN

- Spelling words with open syllables
- Spelling words with vowel **y**
- Spelling words with VCe syllables

DAILY PAGE GOALS

Day	Complete	Day	Complete	Day	Complete
1	ii–6	7	32–37	13	63–68
2	7–14	8	38–44	14	69–76
3	15–20	9	45–51	15	77–83
4	21–25	10	52–56	16	84–89
5	26–27	11	57–58	17	90–91
6	28–31	12	59–62	18	92–96

SKUNK 246

SKUNK

Teacher reads all pages to the learners.

Everyday Words

Set a timer and read the words.

Many words in this Unit are everyday words.

a	the	we	I
my	by	so	go
no	try	why	made
name	like	time	home
use	white		

Time: _____

Circle the hidden words.

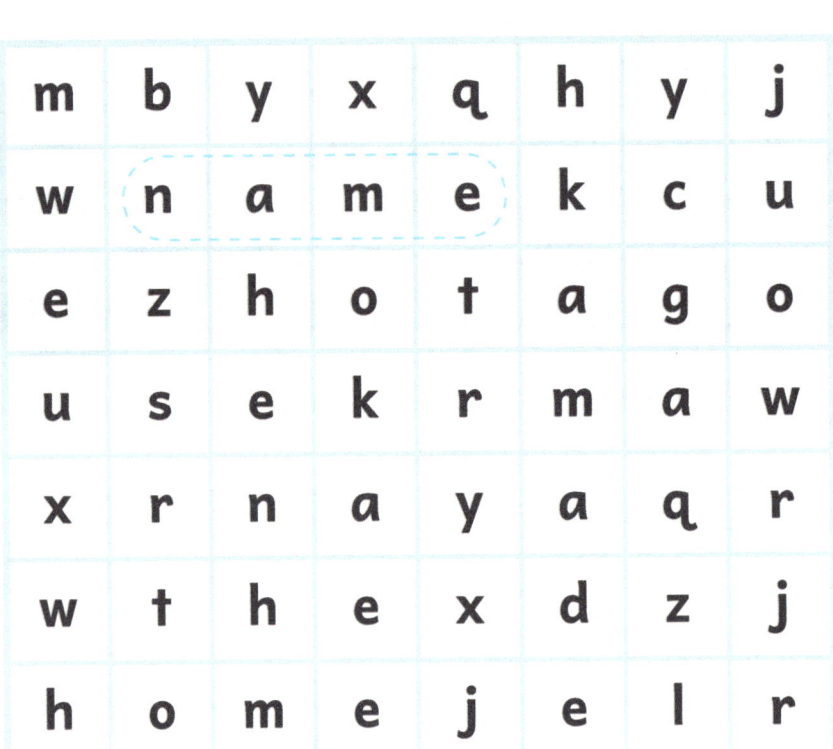

m	b	y	x	q	h	y	j
w	n	a	m	e	k	c	u
e	z	h	o	t	a	g	o
u	s	e	k	r	m	a	w
x	r	n	a	y	a	q	r
w	t	h	e	x	d	z	j
h	o	m	e	j	e	l	r

Word List

name	by	use
home	go	try
made	we	the

Learn:

- Identify open and closed syllables.
- Spell and read words from List 4.

WRITING PHONOGRAM REVIEW

 **Listen to and write the phonograms.**
Underline any multi-letter phonograms.

WORKING WITH WORDS
The words in List 4 are open syllables.

me   he   she

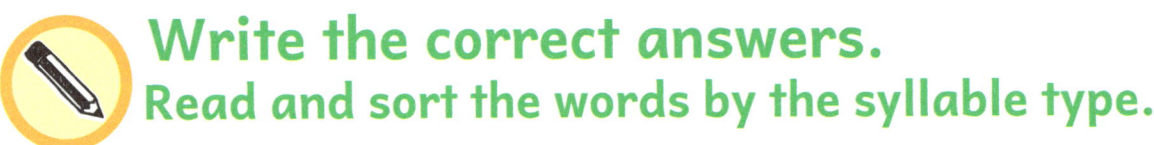 **Write the correct answers.**
Read and sort the words by the syllable type.

hi	hit	pro	prod
she	shell	sky	skim

1)   **Open**   **2)**   **Closed**

Listen!

 **Circle the correct answers.**

3) | syllables | 1 | 2 | 3 | 4 |

4) | sounds | 1 | 2 | 3 | 4 |

✏️ **Write and read.**

5)

 **Choose the correct answer.**

6) What is the syllable type?
   - ○ closed
   - ○ open
   - ○ VCe

Listen!

 **Circle the correct answers.**

| 7) | syllables | 1 | 2 | 3 | 4 |

| 8) | sounds | 1 | 2 | 3 | 4 |

 **Write and read.**

9) _____

 **Choose the correct answer.**

10) The vowel sound is ____.
   ○ r-controlled
   ○ short
   ○ long

Listen!

 Circle the correct answers.

11) | syllables | 1 | 2 | 3 | 4 |

12) | sounds | 1 | 2 | 3 | 4 |

 Write and read.

13) _____

 Choose the correct answer.

14) The vowel sound is ____.
   ○ long
   ○ short
   ○ r-controlled

 **Choose the correct answers.**

15) Which word begins with a consonant digraph?

○ a   ○ the   ○ we

16) Mark (☒) TWO words that have the same vowel sound.

□ a   □ the   □ we

Write the correct answers.
Complete the sentences.

a	we	the

17) After dinner, _____ sit on the porch.

18) I like to look at _____ stars.

19) You can make _____ wish on a shooting star!

SCORE   CORRECT   RESCORE

Learn:

- Read contractions with long vowel sounds.

- Spell and read words from List 4.

WRITING PHONOGRAM REVIEW

 **Listen to and write the phonograms.**
Underline any multi-letter phonograms.

WORKING WITH WORDS

Many contractions begin with a pronoun. The pronouns keep their vowel sounds. They do not change.

$$I + am \longrightarrow I'm$$
$$He + is \longrightarrow He's$$
$$She + will \longrightarrow She'll$$
$$They + had \longrightarrow They'd$$

Write the correct answers.
Complete the sentences.

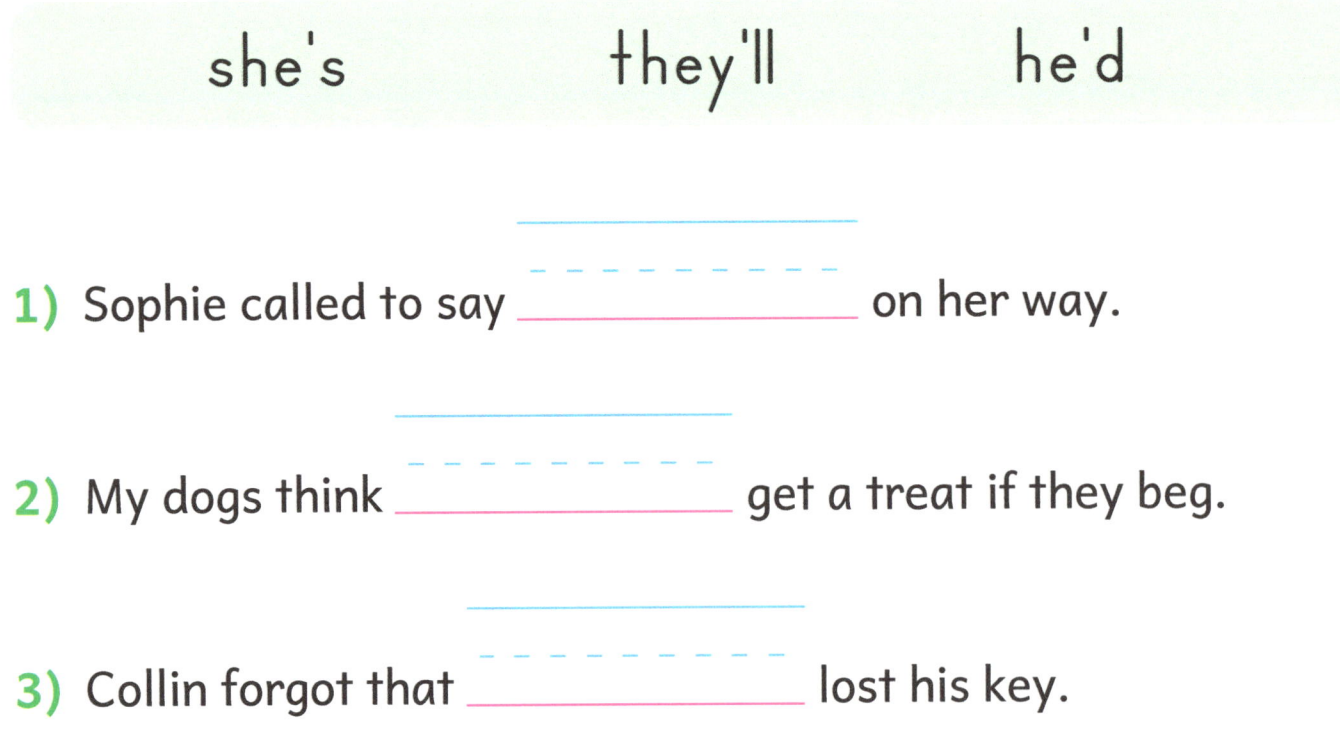

| she's | they'll | he'd |

1) Sophie called to say _____ on her way.

2) My dogs think _____ get a treat if they beg.

3) Collin forgot that _____ lost his key.

8

Listen!

 **Circle the correct answers.**

4)	syllables	1	2	3	4

5)	sounds	1	2	3	4

 **Write and read.**

6) _____

 **Choose the correct answer.**

7) What is the syllable type?
   ○ VCe
   ○ open
   ○ r-controlled

Listen!

? **Circle the correct answers.**

| 8) | syllables | 1 | 2 | 3 | 4 |

| 9) | sounds | 1 | 2 | 3 | 4 |

Write and read.

10) _____

? **Choose the correct answer.**

11) Which reading rule does this word follow?

○ 1ˢᵗ sound of **oo**

○ 4ᵗʰ sound of **y**

○ 3ʳᵈ sound of **y**

Listen!

 **Circle the correct answers.**

| 12) | syllables | 1 | 2 | 3 | 4 |

| 13) | sounds | 1 | 2 | 3 | 4 |

 **Write and read.**

14) _____

 **Choose the correct answer.**

15) The vowel sound is ____.
   ○ long
   ○ short
   ○ r-controlled

Listen!

 **Circle the correct answers.**

16)	syllables	1	2	3	4

17)	sounds	1	2	3	4

 **Write and read.**

18) _____

 **Choose the correct answer.**

19) Which reading rule does this word follow?
- ○ 1st sound of **oo**
- ○ 4th sound of **y**
- ○ 3rd sound of **y**

 **Choose the correct answer.**

20) Which word is always capitalized?

    ○ I   ○ my   ○ fly

 **Write the correct answers.**
Sort the words in ABC order.

I	my	by

21) _____

22) _____

23) _____

 **Use the word in your own sentence.**

fly

24) _____

SCORE ◯   CORRECT ◯   RESCORE ◯

ACTIVITY: Open Syllable Nonsense Words

You can read and spell open syllables. Now read these nonsense words.

re	ty	ba	ro	bo
ve	pu	fro	mu	chi
co	twi	de	gra	bli
pre	dy	bu	pho	sta
hu	qui	fa	cly	vu
tri	phe	ca	ke	swy

Learn:

- Read tricky contractions.

- Spell and read words from List 4.

WRITING PHONOGRAM REVIEW

 **Listen to and write the phonograms.**
Underline any multi-letter phonograms.

WORKING WITH WORDS

These two contractions can be tricky. The vowel sounds change.

do + **not** ⟶ do**n't**   will + **not** ⟶ wo**n't**

We **don't** see you.

I **won't** make it until later.

 Underline the correct answers.

1) Hayden (**don't**, **won't**) be in class on Friday.

2) My baby sister yelled, "(**Don't**, **Won't**) go!"

3) Mom (**don't**, **won't**) like it if we get home late.

Listen!

❓ Circle the correct answers.

4)	syllables	1	2	3	4

5)	sounds	1	2	3	4

✏️ Write and read.

6) _____

❓ Choose the correct answer.

7) The vowel sound is ____.
   ○ long
   ○ short
   ○ r-controlled

Listen!

? Circle the correct answers.

8) syllables   1   2   3   4

9) sounds   1   2   3   4

✏ Write and read.

10) _____

? Choose the correct answer.

11) Which reading rule does this word follow?
- ○ beginning **y**
- ○ 1st sound of **g**
- ○ 2nd sound of **g**

Listen!

 **Circle the correct answers.**

| 12) | syllables | 1 | 2 | 3 | 4 |

| 13) | sounds | 1 | 2 | 3 | 4 |

 **Write and read.**

14) _____

 **Choose the correct answer.**

15) What is the syllable type?
- ○ closed
- ○ open
- ○ VCe

16) The boy was **so** happy.

17) That tree has **no** fruit.

18) The green light means that cars can **go**.

SCORE   CORRECT   RESCORE

PHONOGRAM REVIEW

 **Listen to and circle the correct phonograms.**

1)   n   r   wr

2)   g   ng   j

3)   aw   ai   ay

4)   eigh   igh   ai

5)   ar   ear   er

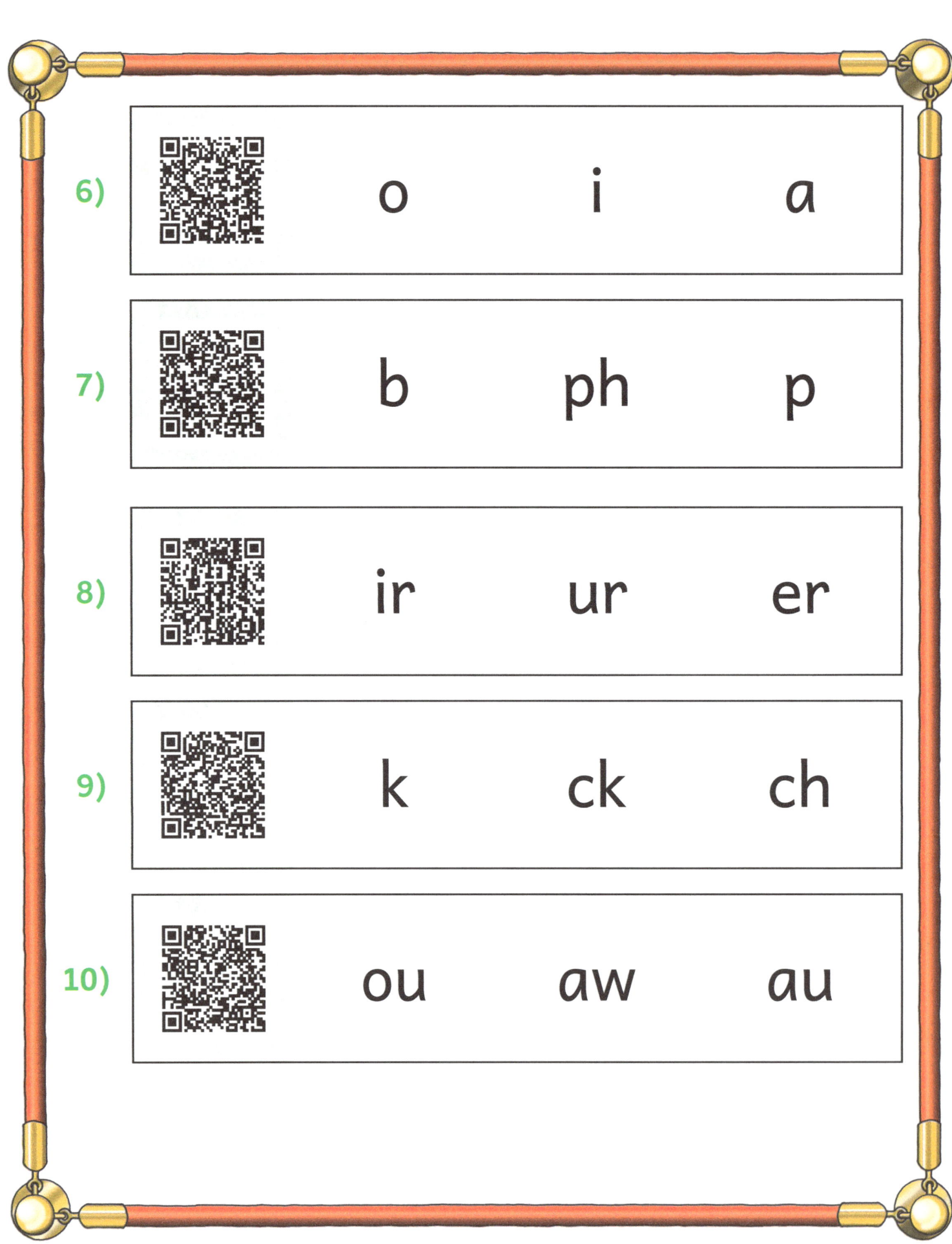

6) o   i   a

7) b   ph   p

8) ir   ur   er

9) k   ck   ch

10) ou   aw   au

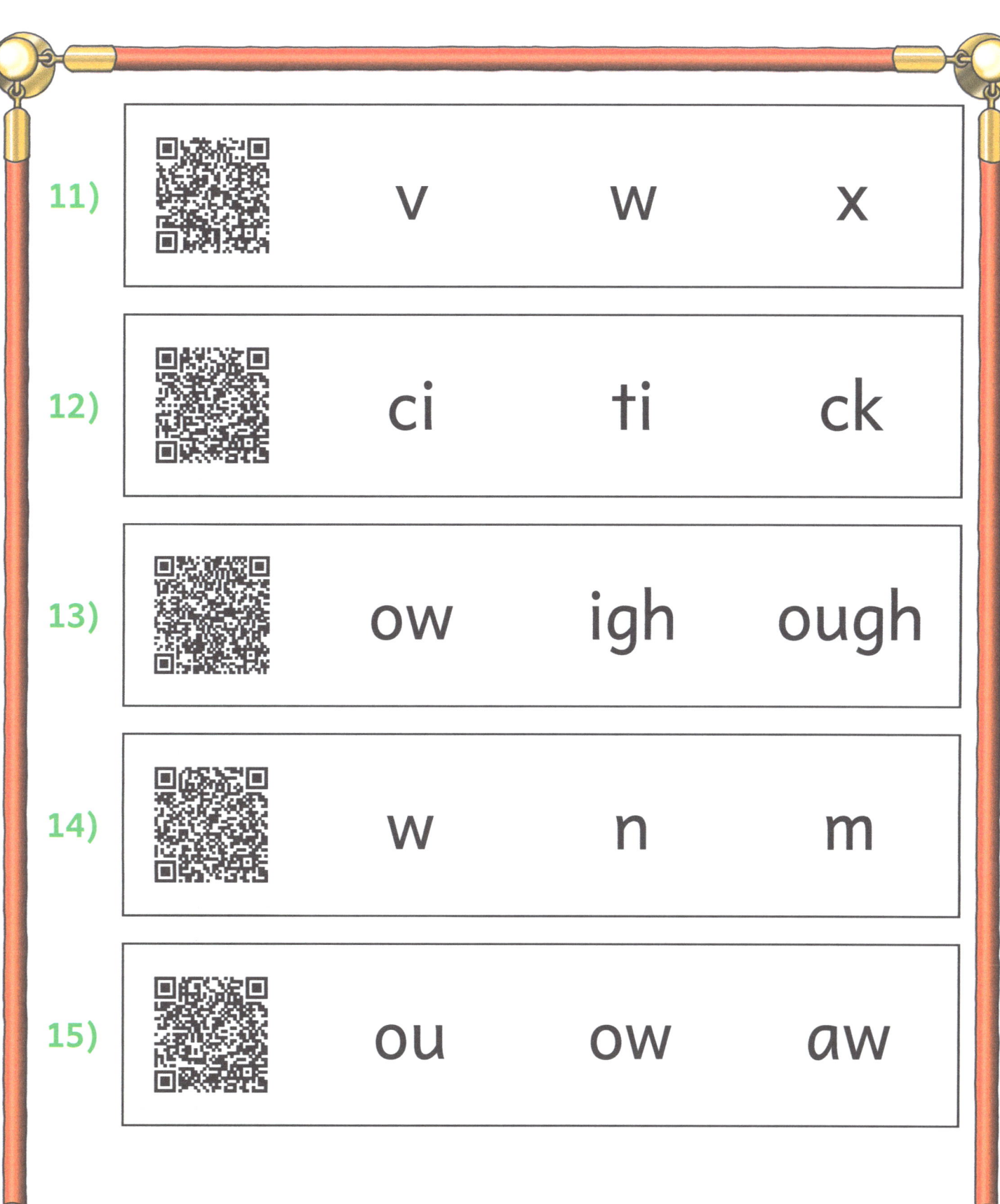

11) v   w   x

12) ci   ti   ck

13) ow   igh   ough

14) w   n   m

15) ou   ow   aw

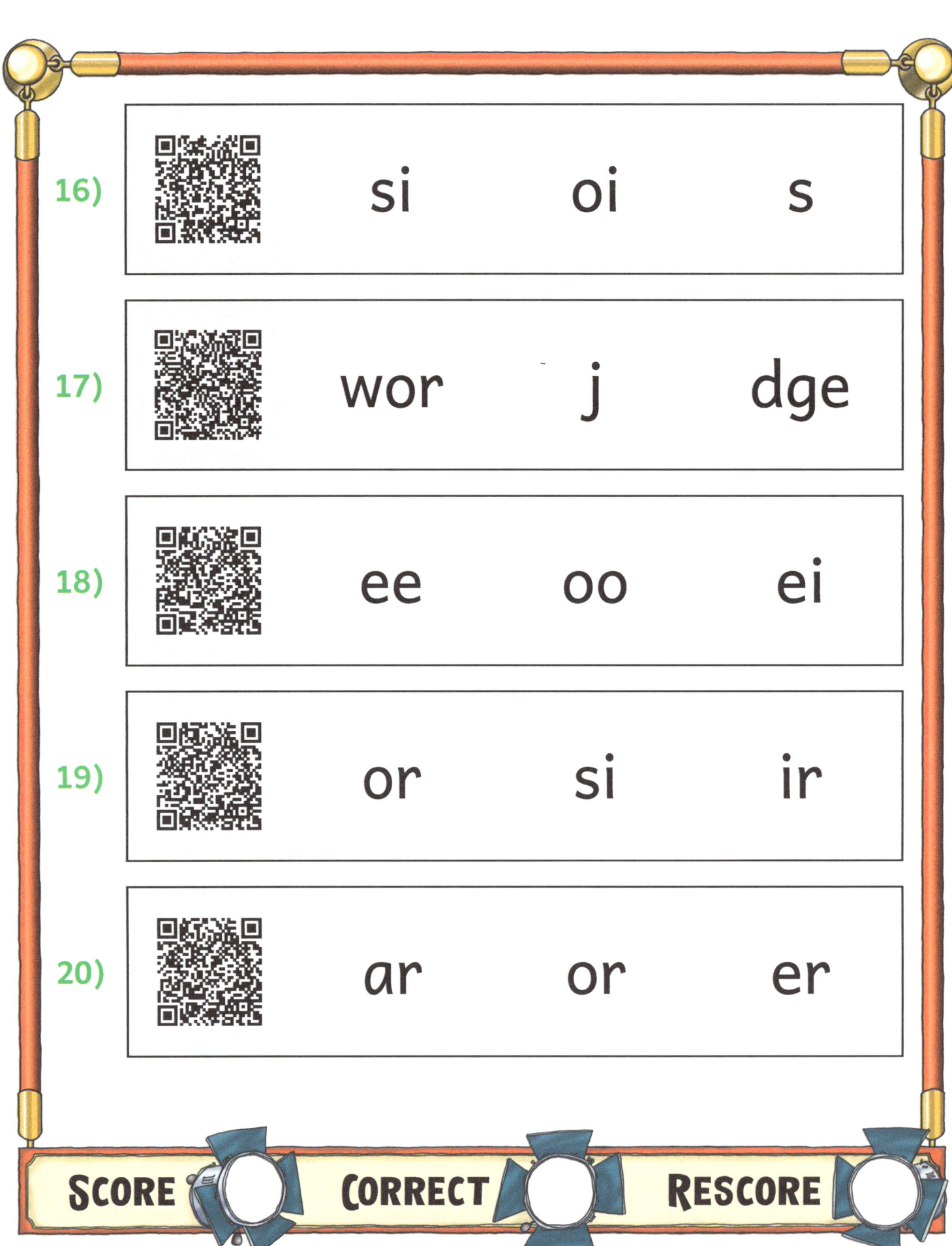

16) si   oi   s

17) wor   j   dge

18) ee   oo   ei

19) or   si   ir

20) ar   or   er

SCORE   CORRECT   RESCORE

SPELLING LIST 4 REVIEW

 Write the correct answers.
Sort the words in ABC order.

a	the	we	I	my
by	fly	so	go	no

1) _____

2) _____

3) _____

4) _____

5) _____

6) _____

7) _____

8) _____

9) _____

10) _____

READER 11: "Kit and the Kite"

This Reader has the tricky word *bye*.
The letter **y** makes its third vowel sound.
The letter **e** is silent.

Tricky Word
bye

 **Listen to the word *bye* in this sentence.**

It is good manners to say "Thank you" and
"**Bye**" when it is time to go.

 **Circle the correct answers.**

1) Mark (☒) TWO words that rhyme with *bye*.
   ☐ tree
   ☐ fly
   ☐ sky

Time to Read!

Reader 11
Kit and the Kite

 **Choose the correct answers.**

2) What was wrong with the bird?
- ○ It did not know how to fly.
- ○ It was stuck in the tree.
- ○ It was scared of the water.

3) How did Kit help the bird?
- ○ She sent her kite up to the bird.
- ○ She climbed the tree to get the bird.
- ○ She made lunch for it.

4) Where did the bird go at the end?
- ○ It swam in the water.
- ○ It ate lunch.
- ○ It flew home.

5) How many syllables are in the word *baby*?
- ○ 1
- ○ 2
- ○ 3

Phonogram Test 16

Listen to and write the correct phonograms.
Underline any multi-letter phonograms.

1)

2)

3)

4)

5)

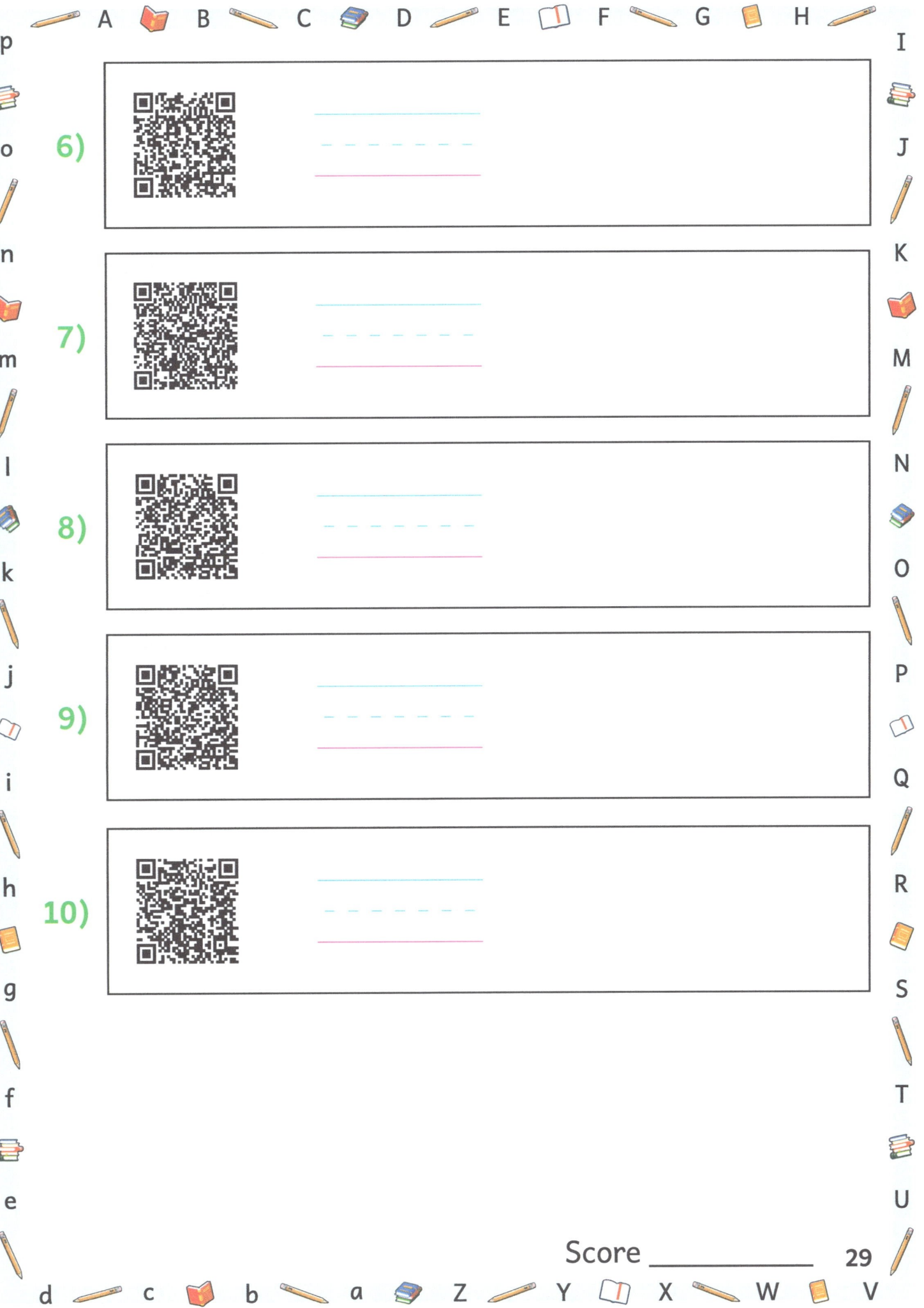

Spelling Test List 4

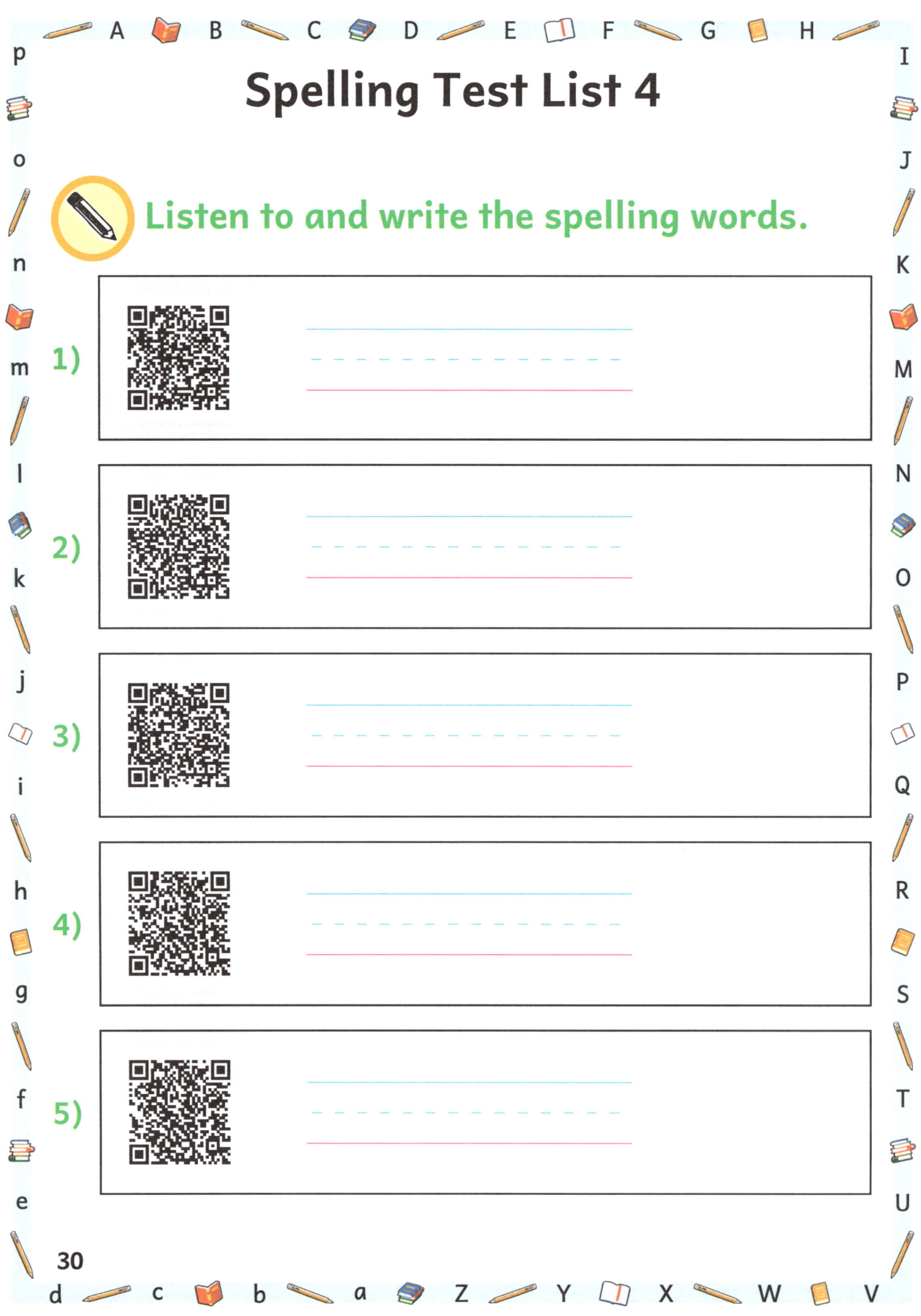

Listen to and write the spelling words.

1)

2)

3)

4)

5)

30

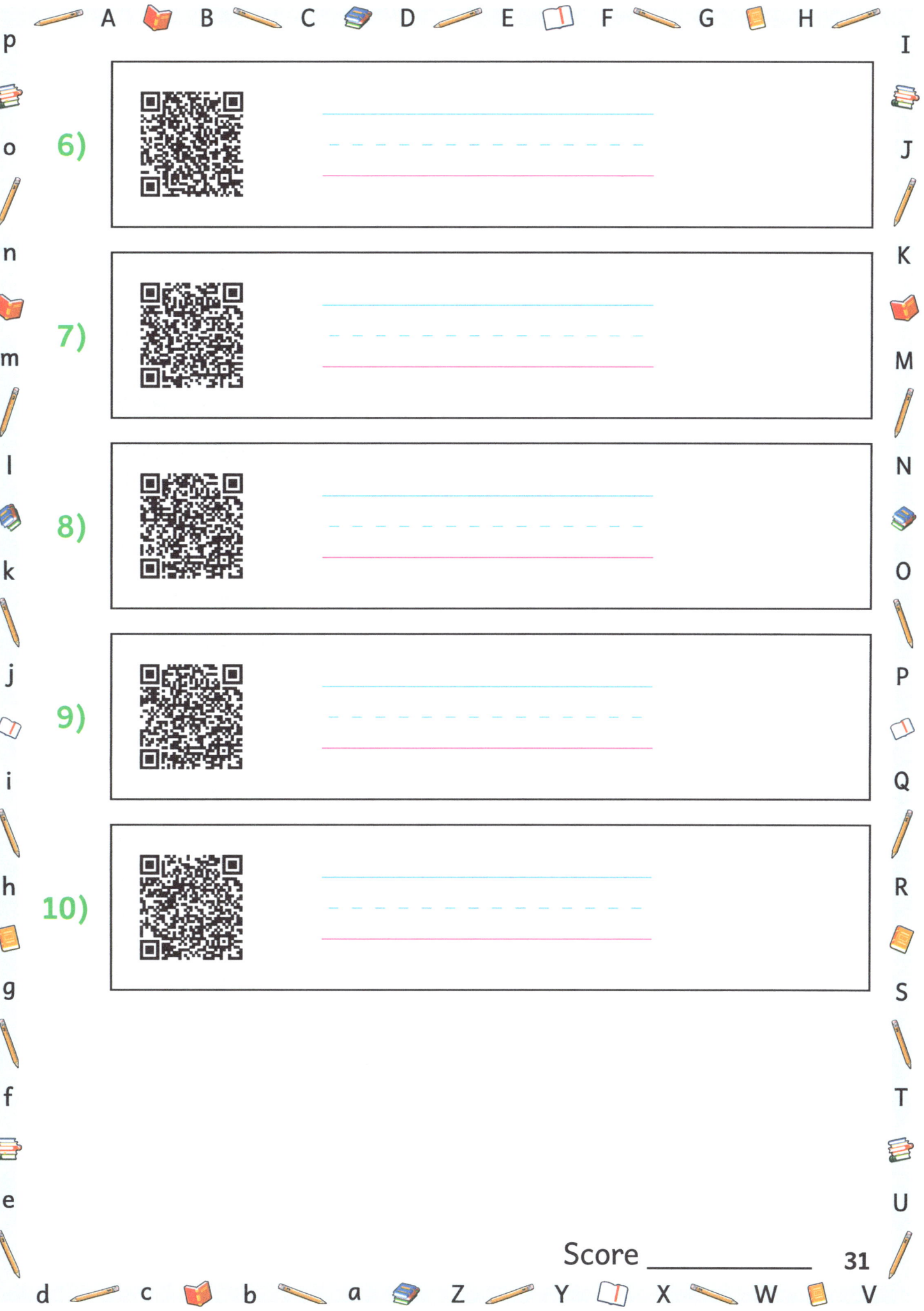

4. SPELLING LIST 5: Part 1

Learn:

- Read and sort words that end with vowel **y**.

- Spell and read words from List 5.

WRITING PHONOGRAM REVIEW

Listen to and write the phonograms.
Underline any multi-letter phonograms.

WORKING WITH WORDS

The words in List 5 end with the letter **y**.

3rd Sound of **y**

cr**y**

4th Sound of **y**

happ**y**

Write the correct answers.
Read and sort the words by the sound of **y**.

| fry | baby | lucky | shy |
| belly | cry | tidy | dry |

1) **3rd Sound of y**

2) **4th Sound of y**

Listen!

Circle the correct answer.

3) syllables 1 2 3 4

Circle the correct answers.
Then, write each syllable.

4)

syllable 1
sounds 1 2 3 4
_____
- - - - - - - - - -
_____

5)
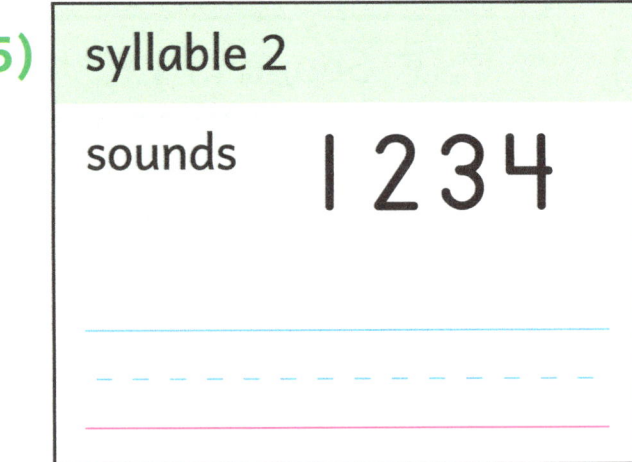
syllable 2
sounds 1 2 3 4
_____
- - - - - - - - - -
_____

 **Write and read.**

_____
- - - - - - - - - -
6) _____

Listen!

❓ Circle the correct answer.

7) | syllables | 1 2 3 4 |

❓ Circle the correct answers.
Then, write each syllable.

8) | syllable 1 |
sounds 1 2 3 4

9) | syllable 2 |
sounds 1 2 3 4

✏ Write and read.

10)

Listen!

? Circle the correct answer.

11)
syllables	1	2	3	4

? Circle the correct answers.
Then, write each syllable.

12)
syllable 1	
sounds	1 2 3 4

13)
syllable 2	
sounds	1 2 3 4

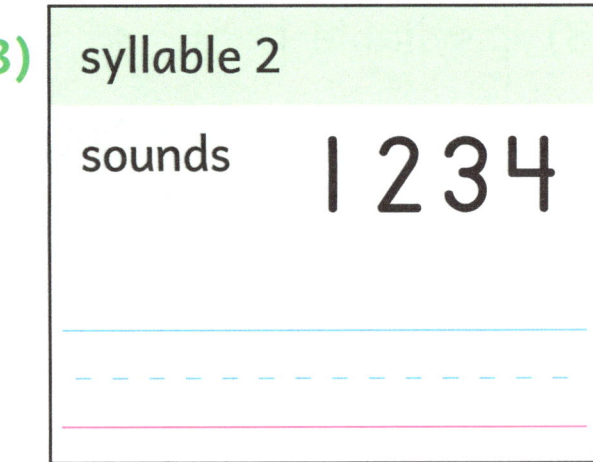

✏️ **Write and read.**

14) _____

 **Circle the correct answers.**
Which picture describes the sentence?

15) The toy costs **fifty** cents.

16) I like to fly my kite on **windy** days.

17) Amy got a **candy** bar.

SCORE   CORRECT   RESCORE

Learn:

- Divide and read two-syllable words.
- Spell and read words from List 5.

WRITING PHONOGRAM REVIEW

 **Listen to and write the phonograms.**
Underline any multi-letter phonograms.

WORKING WITH WORDS

 **Mark, divide, and read the words.**
Underline the multi-letter phonograms. Circle the
syllable division pattern. Write each syllable.

Word	Pattern	Syllable 1	Syllable 2
1) gup|py	VCV (VCCV)	gup	py
2) ivy	VCV / VCCV		
3) penny	VCV / VCCV		
4) derby	VCV / VCCV		
5) rowdy	VCV / VCCV		
6) county	VCV / VCCV		

Listen!

? **Circle the correct answers.**

7) | syllables | 1 | 2 | 3 | 4 |

8) | sounds | 1 | 2 | 3 | 4 |

✏️ **Write and read.**

9) _____

? **Choose the correct answer.**

10) Which reading rule does this word follow?
- ○ 4ᵗʰ sound of **y**
- ○ 2ⁿᵈ sound of **c**
- ○ 1ˢᵗ sound of **c**

Listen!

? Circle the correct answers.

11) | syllables | 1 | 2 | 3 | 4 |

12) | sounds | 1 | 2 | 3 | 4 |

✏ Write and read.

13) _____

? Choose the correct answer.

14) What is the syllable type?
   ○ open
   ○ r-controlled
   ○ VCe

Listen!

 **Circle the correct answers.**

15)	syllables	1	2	3	4

16)	sounds	1	2	3	4

 **Write and read.**

17) _____

 **Choose the correct answer.**

18) The vowel sound is ____.
  ○ short
  ○ r-controlled
  ○ long

Listen!

? Circle the correct answers.

| 19) | syllables | 1 | 2 | 3 | 4 |

| 20) | sounds | 1 | 2 | 3 | 4 |

✏ Write and read.

21) _____

? Choose the correct answer.

22) Which reading rule does this word follow?

- ○ double **s**
- ○ beginning **s**
- ○ 1st sound of **c**

Choose the correct answer.

23) Which word begins with a consonant digraph?

    ○ why   ○ sky   ○ try

Write the correct answers.
Sort the words in ABC order.

cry	why	sky

24) _____

25) _____

26) _____

Use the word in your own sentence.

try

27) _____

SCORE   CORRECT   RESCORE

Learn:

- Read sentences with the fourth sound of **y**.

- Spell and read words from List 5.

WRITING PHONOGRAM REVIEW

 **Listen to and write the phonograms.**
Underline any multi-letter phonograms.

WORKING WITH WORDS

 **Read.**

Toby is a fluffy bunny. He has a home in a leafy forest. Last week, Toby went hopping down a twisty, bumpy path. He saw a shiny key. "Wow! What does it unlock?" Toby asked. That's how Toby began his quest.

Toby looked in each nook and cranny of the forest. At last, he saw a rusty box with a great big lock! His paw was shaky, but he put the key in the lock and turned. It clicked! The box sprang open.

 **Circle the correct answers.**

1) Which word describes Toby?

    ○ fluffy   ○ leafy   ○ shiny

2) Which word describes the key?

    ○ fluffy   ○ leafy   ○ shiny

Draw.

3) Draw a picture of what you think was in the box.

Listen!

 **Circle the correct answer.**

4) | syllables | 1   2   3   4 |

 **Circle the correct answers.**
Then, write each syllable.

5) | syllable 1 |
   | sounds | 1 2 3 4 |
   | _____ |
   | _____ |
   | _____ |

6) | syllable 2 |
   | sounds | 1 2 3 4 |
   | _____ |
   | _____ |
   | _____ |

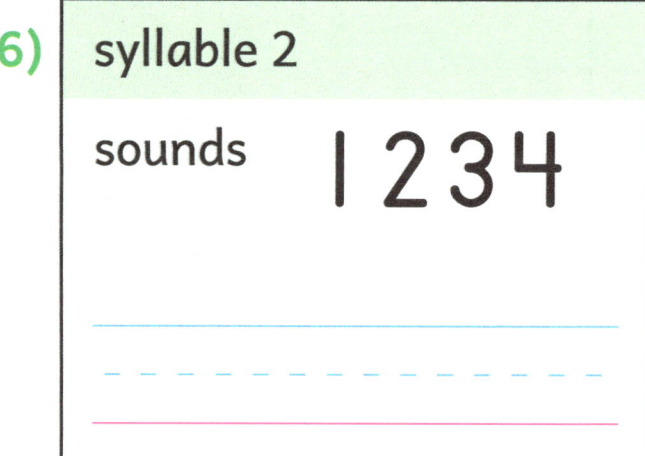 **Write and read.**

_____
_____
7) _____

48

Listen!

? Circle the correct answer.

8) | syllables | 1   2   3   4 |

? Circle the correct answers.
Then, write each syllable.

9)

syllable 1

sounds   1 2 3 4

10)

syllable 2

sounds   1 2 3 4

✏ Write and read.

11) _____

Listen!

 **Circle the correct answer.**

12)
syllables	1	2	3	4

 **Circle the correct answers.**
Then, write each syllable.

13)
syllable 1
sounds   1 2 3 4
_____
- - - - - - - - - - -
_____

14)
syllable 2
sounds   1 2 3 4
_____
- - - - - - - - - - -
_____

 **Write and read.**

_____
- - - - - - - - - - - - - - -
15) _____

Write the correct answers.
Draw a line between the syllables.

16) crazy

17) lady

Write the correct answers.
Complete the sentences.

lady   any   crazy

18) The fair is so crowded and _____.

19) We need to get a map from that _____.

20) I do not see _____ maps.

SCORE   CORRECT   RESCORE

PHONOGRAM REVIEW

 Listen to and circle the correct phonograms.

1)  ph   sh   h

2)  nk   ng   gn

3)  oo   ui   ew

4)  ou   ow   ough

5)  dge   qu   j

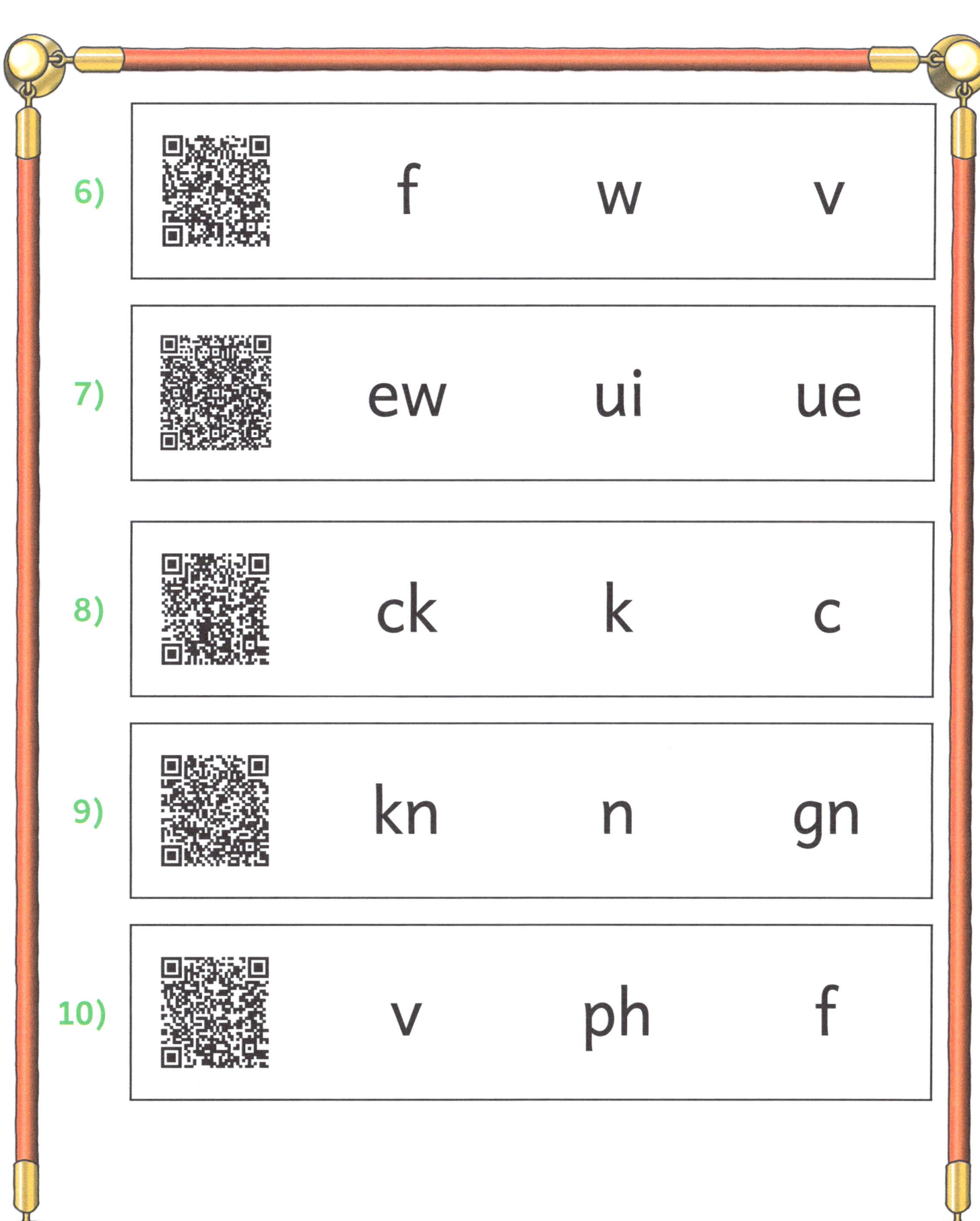

6) f   w   v

7) ew   ui   ue

8) ck   k   c

9) kn   n   gn

10) v   ph   f

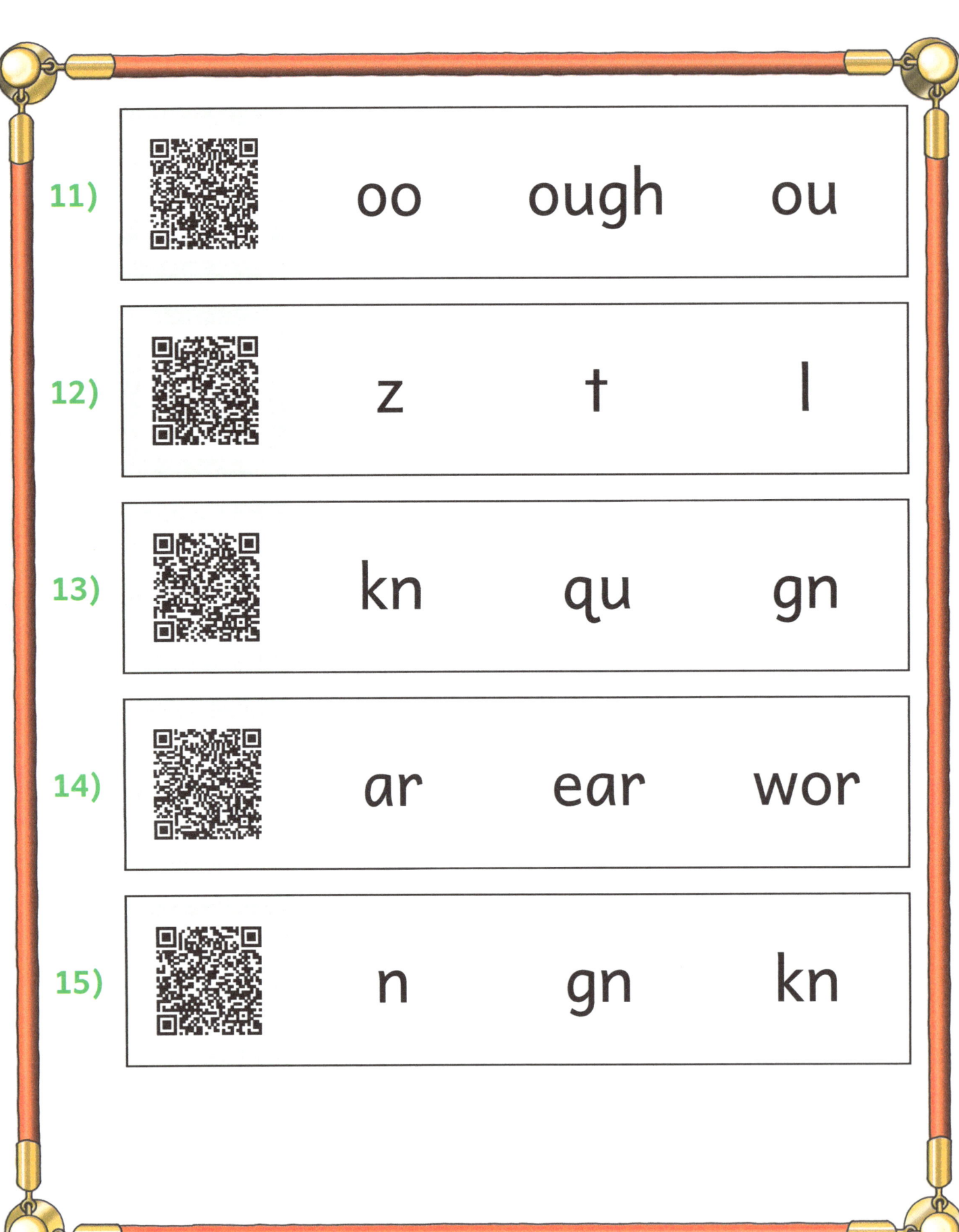

11) oo   ough   ou

12) z   t   l

13) kn   qu   gn

14) ar   ear   wor

15) n   gn   kn

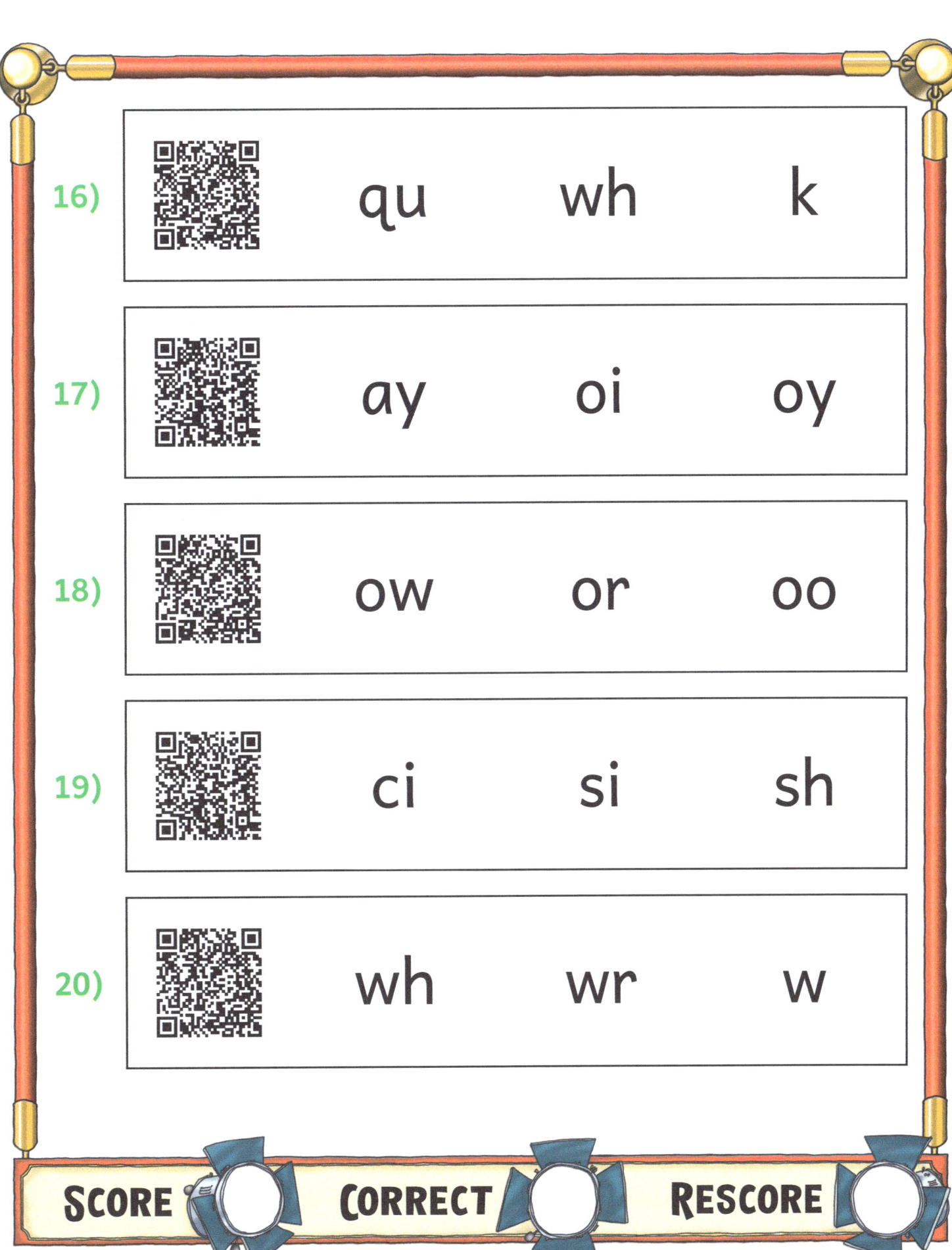

16) qu   wh   k

17) ay   oi   oy

18) ow   or   oo

19) ci   si   sh

20) wh   wr   w

SCORE   CORRECT   RESCORE

SPELLING LIST 5 REVIEW

 **Write the correct answers.**
Sort the words by the number of syllables.

crazy   any   lady   cry   try
why   sky   fifty   windy   candy

1)   1 Syllable   2)   2 Syllables

READER 12: "Crazy Day"

This Reader has the tricky word *many*. The letter **a** makes short **e** sound. It sounds like the word *any*.

 **Listen to the words *any* and *many* in these sentences.**

> The shop has **many** books. You may get **any** book you want.

 **Write the correct answers.**
Complete the sentences.

| of | does | many |

1) This playlist has so ＿＿＿＿＿＿ songs.

2) Do you know any ＿＿＿＿＿＿ them?

3) Abby ＿＿＿＿＿＿ not like rock music.

Reader 12
Crazy Day

? Choose the correct answers.

4) What was one of Zip's problems?
   ○ She lost a contest.
   ○ She did not know how to get home.
   ○ She lost her marker and paper.

5) What does Pip's mom tell him to do when he is sad?
   ○ Think of good things.
   ○ Eat candy.
   ○ Take a long nap.

6) How does Zip feel at the end?
   ○ sad
   ○ mad
   ○ happy

Phonogram Test 17

Listen to and write the correct phonograms.
Underline any multi-letter phonograms.

1)

2)

3)

4)

5)

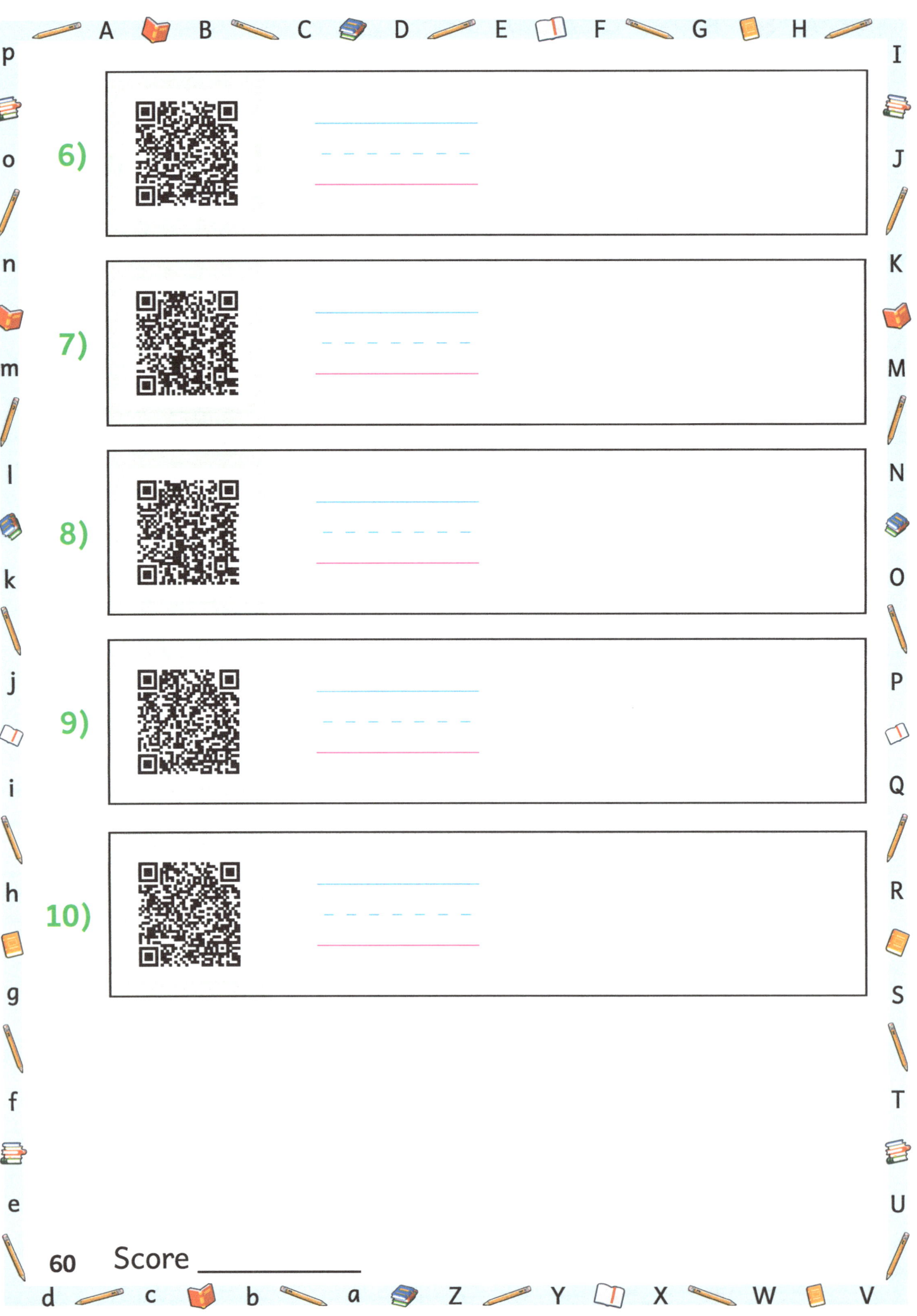

A B C D E F G H I J K L M N O P Q R S T U V W X Y Z

6)

7)

8)

9)

10)

60   Score _____

Spelling Test List 5

Listen to and write the spelling words.

1)

2)

3)

4)

5)

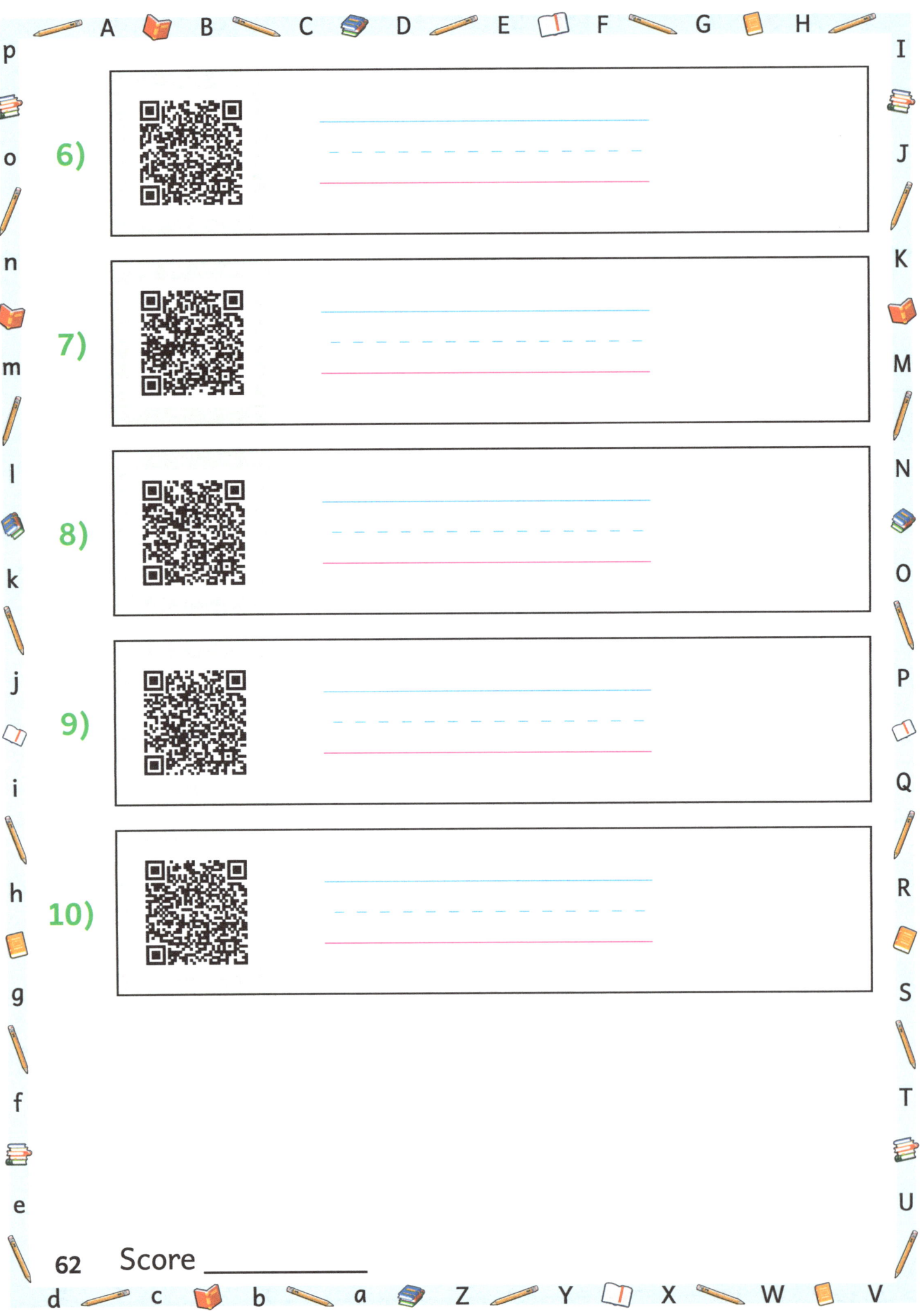

6)

7)

8)

9)

10)

Score _____

Learn:

- Identify open, closed, and VCe syllables.

- Spell and read words from List 6.

WRITING PHONOGRAM REVIEW

 **Listen to and write the phonogram.**
Underline any multi-letter phonograms.

WORKING WITH WORDS

The words in List 6 are VCe syllables. The silent final **e** makes vowels say their long sounds. The silent final **e** has many jobs. This is its first job.

Silent Final e Job: Vowel Boss

Makes vowels say their long sounds in VCe syllables.

name   **Mike**

 **Write the correct answers.**
Read and sort the words by the syllable type.

the	them	these	no	nod
note	spy	spin	spike	

1) **Closed**   2) **Open**   3) **VCe**

Listen!

 **Circle the correct answers.**

4)	syllables	1	2	3	4

5)	sounds	1	2	3	4

 **Write and read.**

6) _____

 **Choose the correct answer.**

7) The vowel sound is _____.
  ○ long
  ○ r-controlled
  ○ short

? **Circle the correct answers.**

8)	syllables	1	2	3	4

9)	sounds	1	2	3	4

✏️ **Write and read.**

10) _____

? **Choose the correct answer.**

11) The last letter is ____.
   ○ silent
   ○ a consonant
   ○ voiced

Listen!

 **Circle the correct answers.**

12)	syllables	1	2	3	4

13)	sounds	1	2	3	4

 **Write and read.**

14) _____

 **Choose the correct answer.**

15) What is the syllable type?
- ○ closed
- ○ open
- ○ VCe

 ## Choose the correct answers.

16) Mark (☒) TWO words that have the same vowel sound.

☐ made   ☐ name   ☐ like

 ## Write the correct answers.
Complete the sentences.

like	made	name

17) The _____ of the show is *Tiny Tales*.

18) We _____ to eat popcorn when we watch it.

19) Last night, we also _____ cookies.

SCORE   CORRECT   RESCORE

Learn:

- Divide and read two-syllable words that end with a VCe syllable.

- Spell and read words from List 6.

WRITING PHONOGRAM REVIEW

 **Listen to and write the phonograms.**
Underline any multi-letter phonograms.

WORKING WITH WORDS

Reading Rules

Silent final **e**: A final letter **e** is silent when the word has another vowel.

When dividing syllables, do not mark the silent final **e**. You may draw an arrow to help you remember the silent **e** makes the vowel before it long.

$$\underset{\text{Open}}{\text{c}}\ \overset{v}{\text{a}}\ \Big|\ \overset{c}{\text{n}}\ \overset{v}{\text{i}}\ \text{n}\ \underset{\text{VCe}}{\text{e}} \qquad \underset{\text{Closed}}{\text{s}}\ \overset{v}{\text{u}}\ \overset{c}{\text{p}}\ \Big|\ \overset{c}{\text{p}}\ \overset{v}{\text{o}}\ \text{s}\ \underset{\text{VCe}}{\text{e}}$$

v	c v		v c	c v
c a	n i n e		s u p	p o s e
Open	VCe		Closed	VCe

 **Mark, divide, and read the VCV and VCCV words.**

beside	ignite	unite	advice
donate	decide	mandate	female
sublime	profile	rotate	dispute

70

 **Circle the correct answers.**

1)	syllables	1	2	3	4

2)	sounds	1	2	3	4

 **Write and read.**

3) _____

 **Choose the correct answer.**

4) What is the syllable type?
- ○ VCe
- ○ r-controlled
- ○ open

Listen!

 **Circle the correct answers.**

| 5) | syllables | 1 | 2 | 3 | 4 |

| 6) | sounds | 1 | 2 | 3 | 4 |

 **Write and read.**

7) _____

 **Choose the correct answer.**

8) The vowel sound is _____.
   ○ short
   ○ r-controlled
   ○ long

Listen!

 **Circle the correct answers.**

| 9) | syllables | 1 | 2 | 3 | 4 |

| 10) | sounds | 1 | 2 | 3 | 4 |

 **Write and read.**

11) _____

 **Choose the correct answer.**

12) The last letter is ____.
- ○ a consonant
- ○ silent
- ○ voiced

Listen!

 **Circle the correct answers.**

| 13) | syllables | 1 | 2 | 3 | 4 |

| 14) | sounds | 1 | 2 | 3 | 4 |

 **Write and read.**

15) _____

 **Choose the correct answer.**

16) What is the syllable type?
   ○ VCe
   ○ closed
   ○ vowel team

❓ Choose the correct answers.

17) Mark (☒) TWO words that have the same vowel sound.

☐ rode   ☐ home   ☐ use

✏️ Write the correct answers.
Sort the words in ABC order.

time	rode	use

18) _____

19) _____

20) _____

✏️ Use the word in your own sentence.

home

21) _____

SCORE   CORRECT   RESCORE

ACTIVITY: VCe Nonsense Words

You can read and spell VCe syllables. Now read these nonsense words.

vate	jite	bobe	shole	fide
ote	nade	fime	zike	habe
yate	prine	zame	chate	upe
phome	lebe	slipe	grote	fale
cive	brote	zoke	jame	stoze
yede	trive	knime	ake	frice

9. SPELLING LIST 6: Part 3

Learn:

- Divide and read two-syllable words.
- Spell and read words from List 6.

WRITING PHONOGRAM REVIEW

 **Listen to and write the phonograms.**
Underline any multi-letter phonograms.

WORKING WITH WORDS

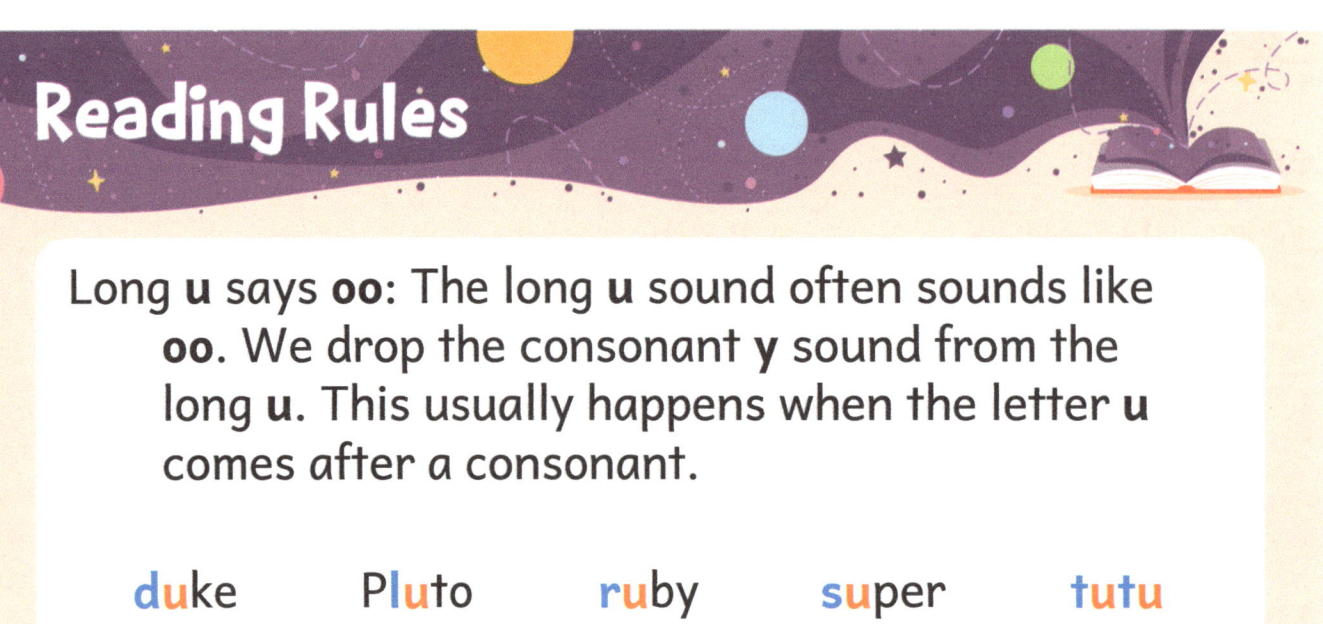

Reading Rules

Long **u** says **oo**: The long **u** sound often sounds like **oo**. We drop the consonant **y** sound from the long **u**. This usually happens when the letter **u** comes after a consonant.

duke   P**lu**to   **ru**by   **su**per   **tutu**

Mark, divide, and read the VCV and VCCV words.
Remember, underline the multi-letter phonograms first.

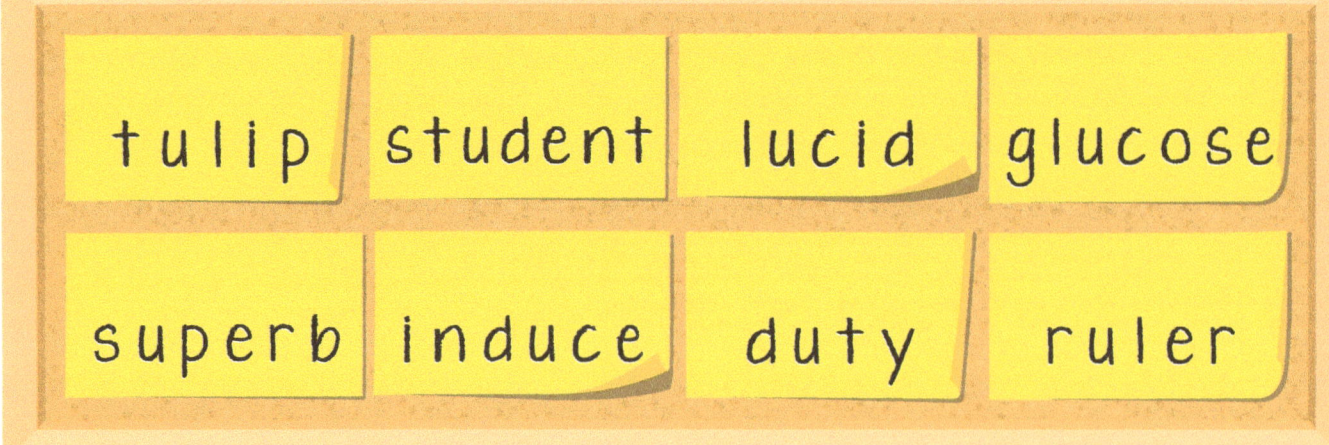

tulip   student   lucid   glucose

superb   induce   duty   ruler

 **Circle the correct answers.**

1) | syllables | 1 | 2 | 3 | 4 |

2) | sounds | 1 | 2 | 3 | 4 |

 **Write and read.**

3) _____

 **Choose the correct answer.**

4) Which reading rule does this word follow?
   - ○ long **u** says **oo**
   - ○ middle **s**
   - ○ 1ˢᵗ sound of **oo**

Listen!

 **Circle the correct answers.**

5) | syllables | 1 2 3 4

6) | sounds | 1 2 3 4

 **Write and read.**

7) _____

 **Choose the correct answer.**

8) The vowel sound is ____.
   ○ short
   ○ long
   ○ r-controlled

Listen!

 **Circle the correct answers.**

| 9) | syllables | 1 | 2 | 3 | 4 |

| 10) | sounds | 1 | 2 | 3 | 4 |

 **Write and read.**

11) _____

 **Choose the correct answer.**

12) What is the syllable type?
- ○ closed
- ○ open
- ○ VCe

 **Choose the correct answers.**

13) Which word is something that tells you how to act?
- ○ rule
- ○ stone
- ○ white

14) Which word is a color?
- ○ rule
- ○ stone
- ○ white

15) Which word means a rock?
- ○ rule
- ○ stone
- ○ white

SCORE ○ CORRECT ○ RESCORE ○

ACTIVITY: Spelling Words

Write the spelling words.

like

name

rode

home

stone

white

PHONOGRAM REVIEW

 Listen to and circle the correct phonograms.

1)  oe   oa   oo

2)  oa   a   oe

3) oo   u   a

4)  l   th   b

5)  th   ei   igh

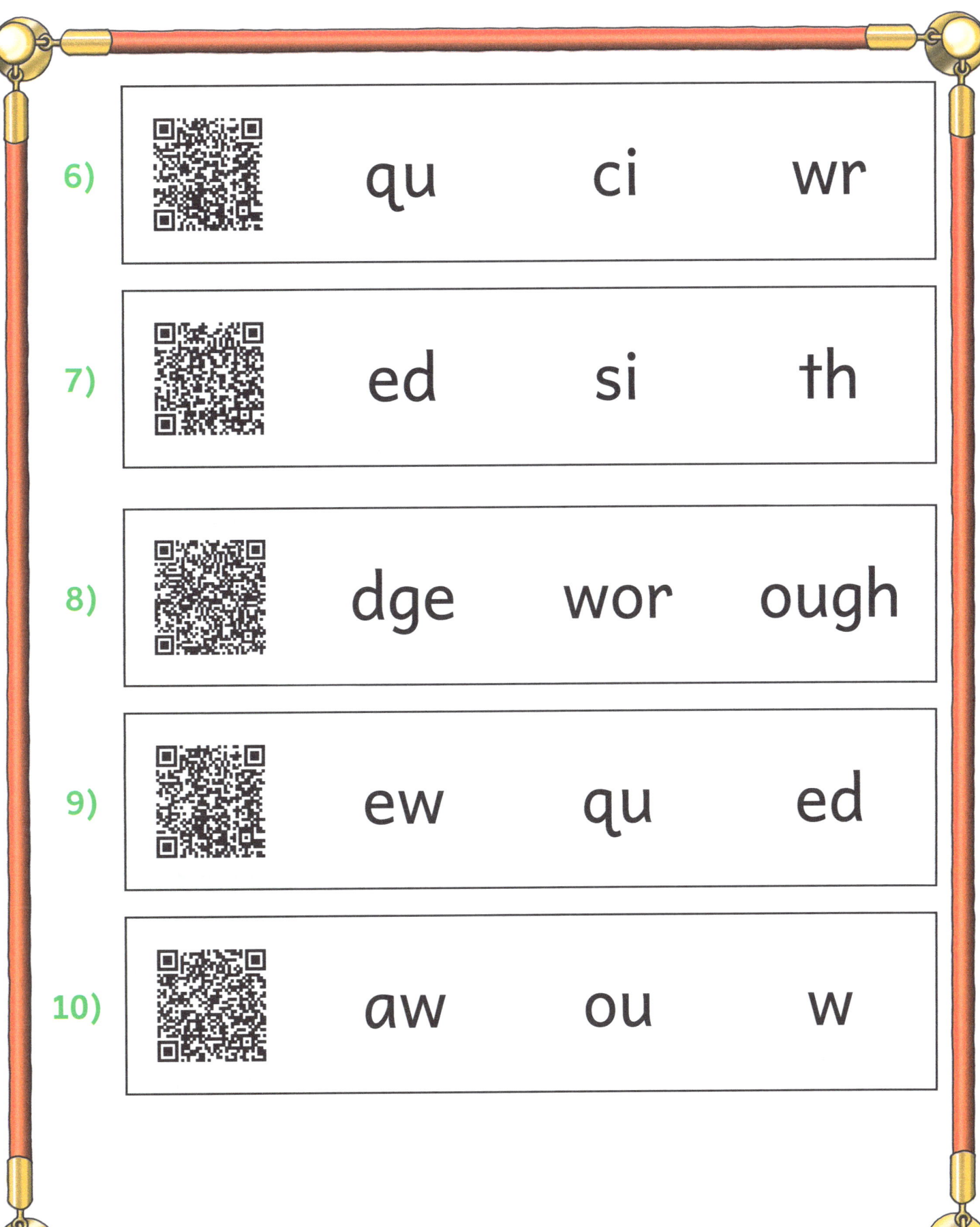

6) qu   ci   wr

7) ed   si   th

8) dge   wor   ough

9) ew   qu   ed

10) aw   ou   w

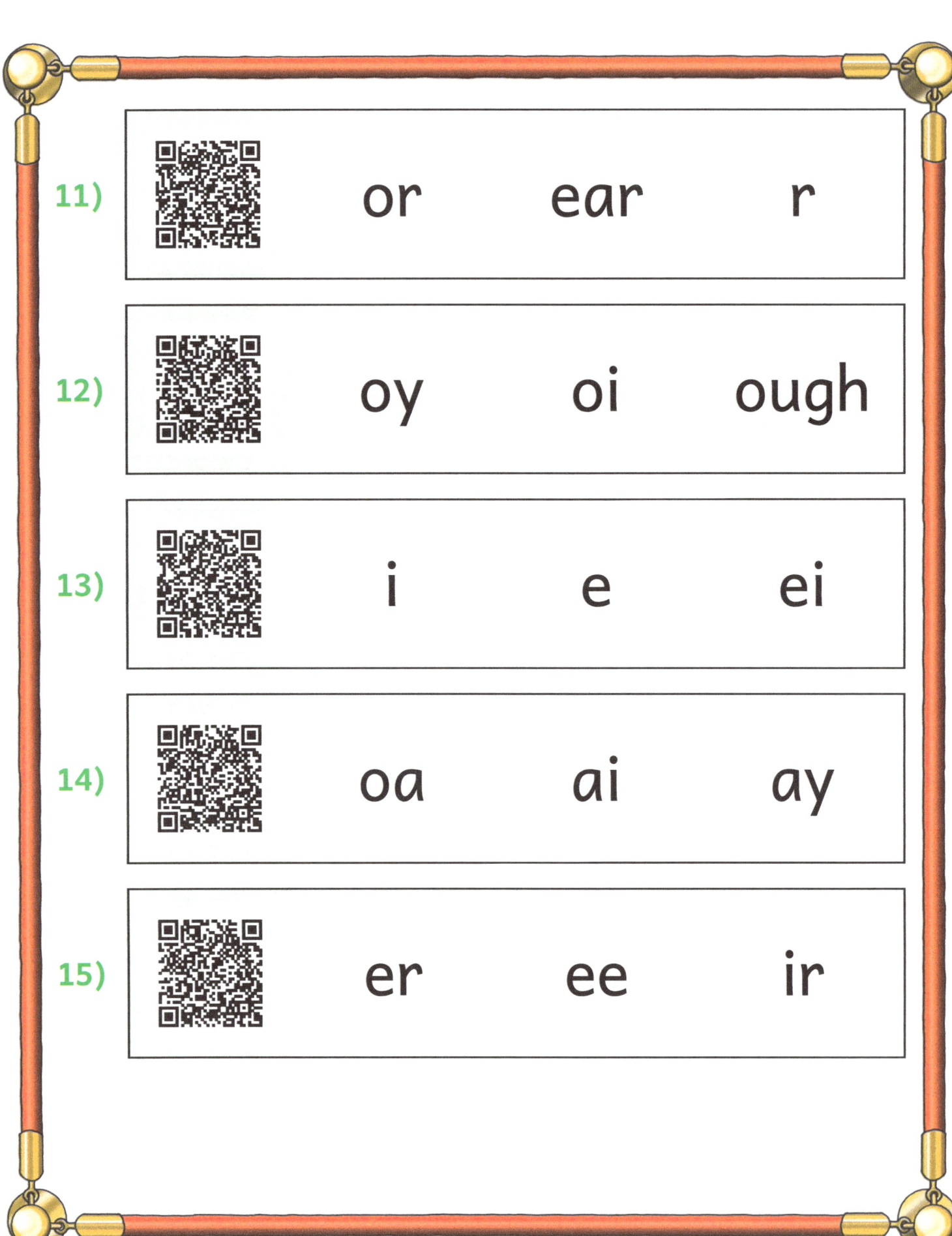

11) or   ear   r

12) oy   oi   ough

13) i   e   ei

14) oa   ai   ay

15) er   ee   ir

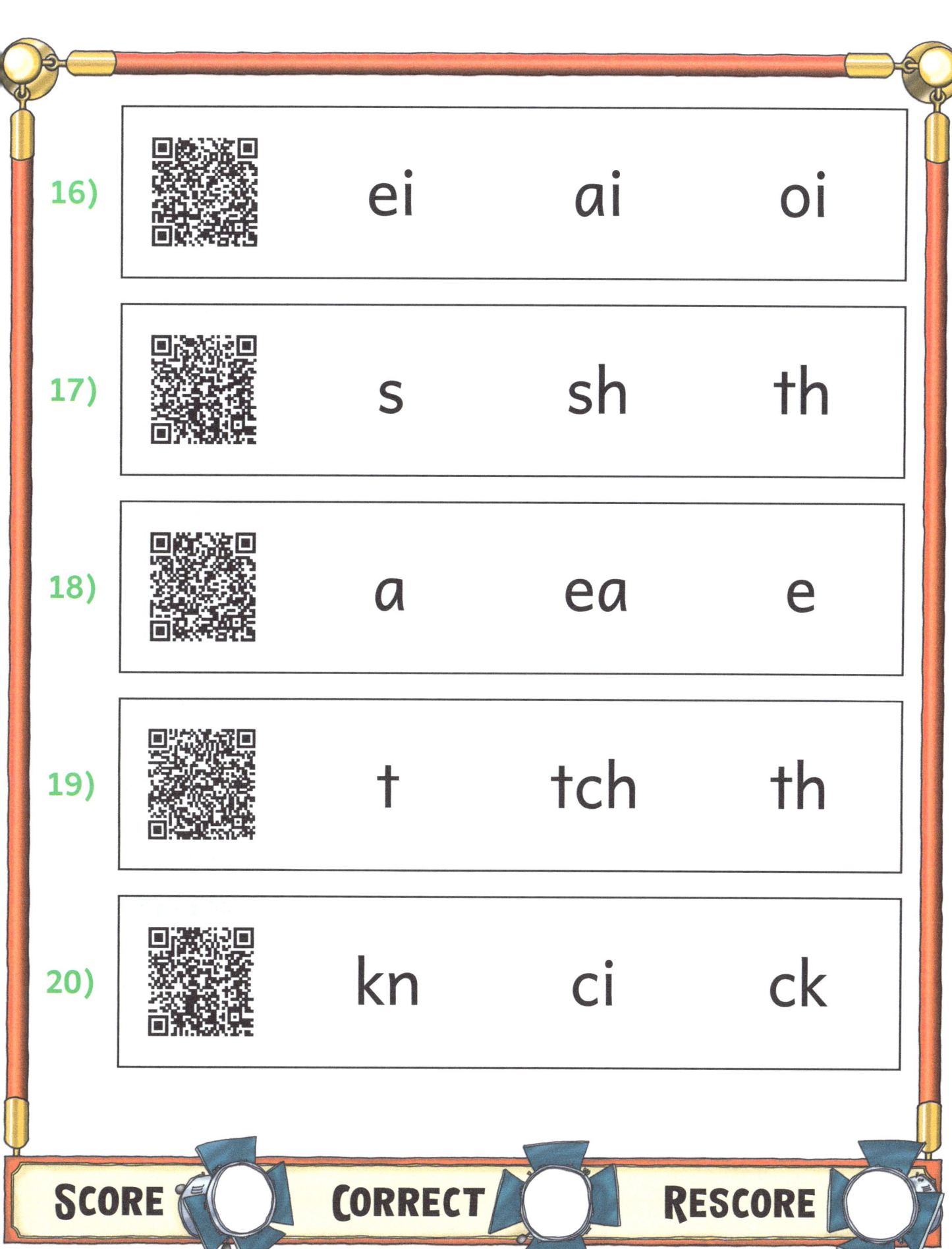

16)   ei   ai   oi

17)   s   sh   th

18)   a   ea   e

19)   t   tch   th

20)   kn   ci   ck

SCORE   CORRECT   RESCORE

SPELLING LIST 6 REVIEW

 **Listen to and circle the correct words.**

1)  like   time   white

2)  rode   use   rule

3)  rule   rode   home

4)  home   like   time

5)  stone   rode   white

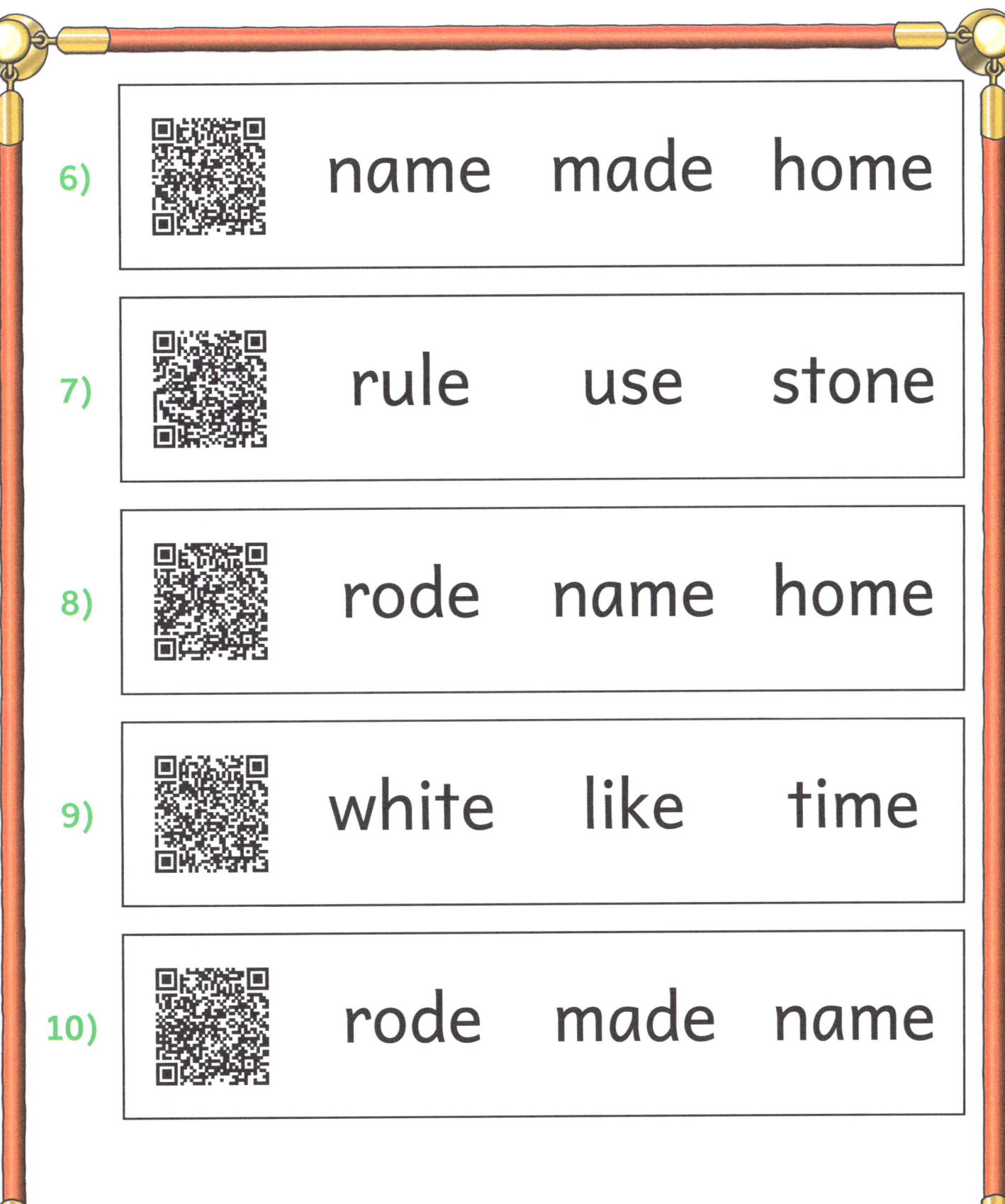

6) name made home

7) rule use stone

8) rode name home

9) white like time

10) rode made name

 **Divide and read the words.**
Remember, underline the multi-letter phonograms first.

1) VCCV

basket   dolphin   under   happy

2) VCV

hermit

3) Compound Words

today   beside   whitefish

Time to Read!

Reader 13
Books at the Beach

 **Choose the correct answers.**

4) What does Kit like to do?

○ cook with her dad

○ swim in the water

○ dig in the sand

5) What did the pals use to carry the books?

○ Kit's bike

○ a car

○ Tug's basket

6) Who did the pals read to?

○ their parents

○ other animals

○ each other

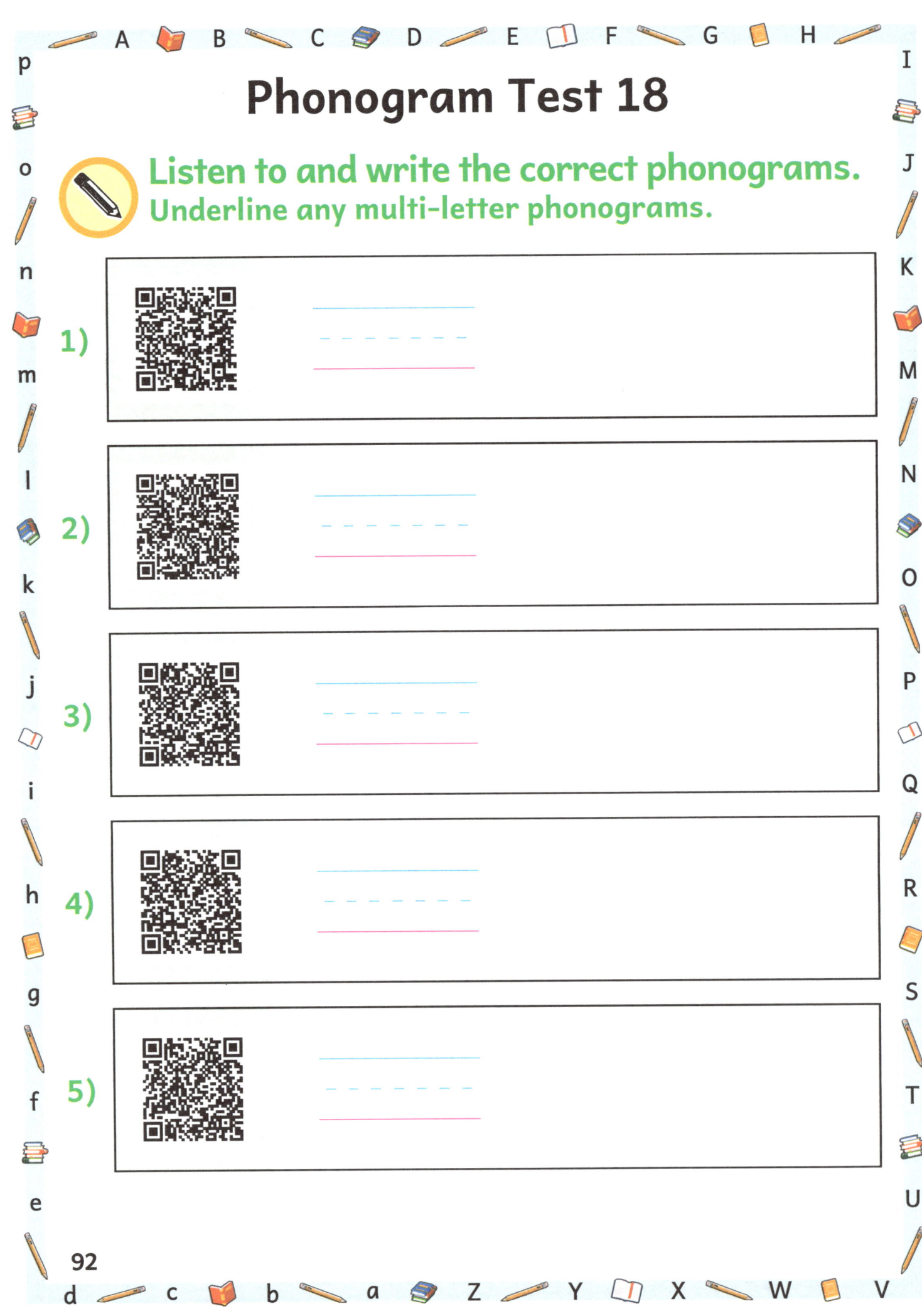

Phonogram Test 18

Listen to and write the correct phonograms.
Underline any multi-letter phonograms.

1)

2)

3)

4)

5)

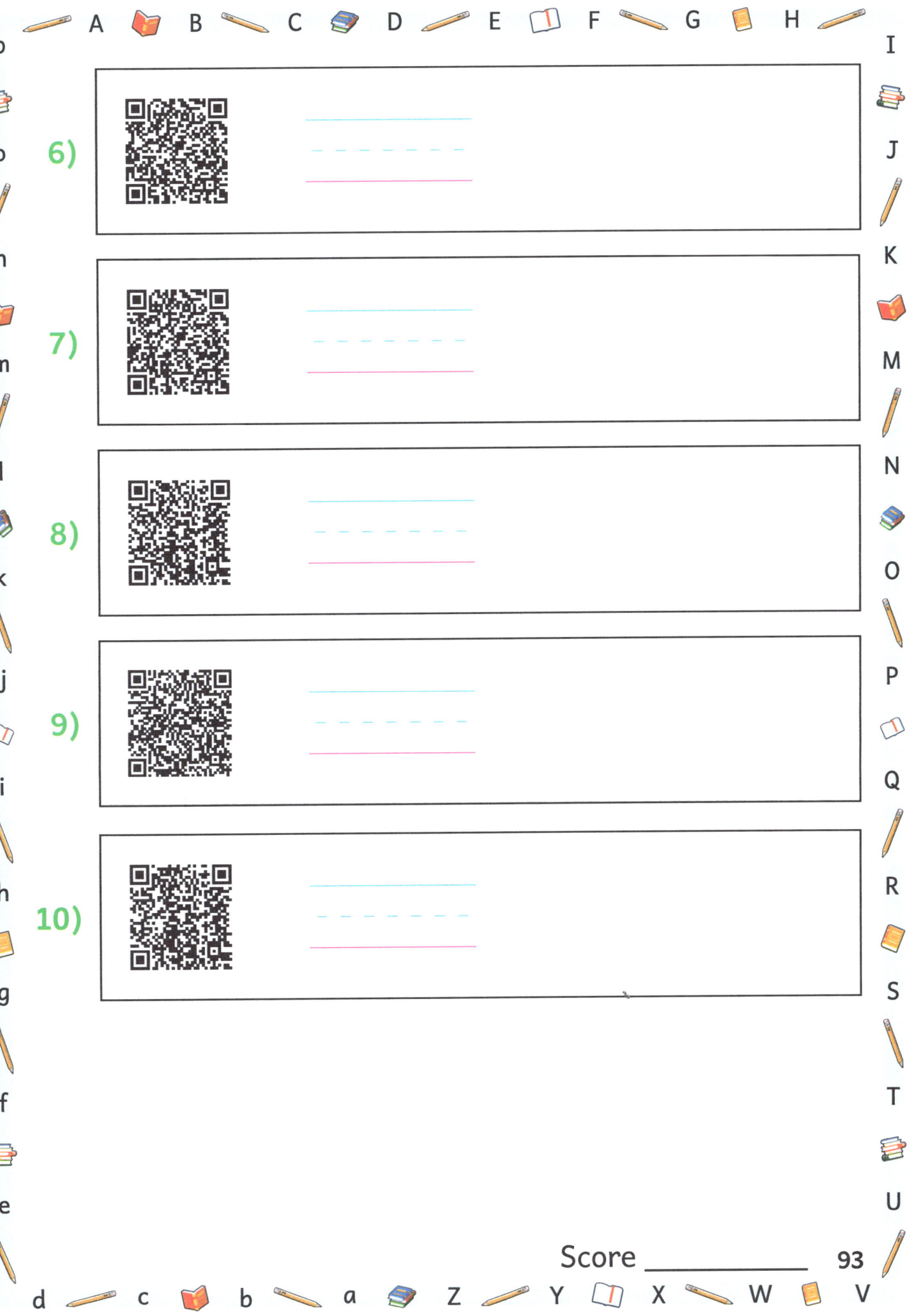

6)

7)

8)

9)

10)

Score _____ 93

Spelling Test List 6

Listen to and write the spelling words.

1)

2)

3)

4)

5)

94

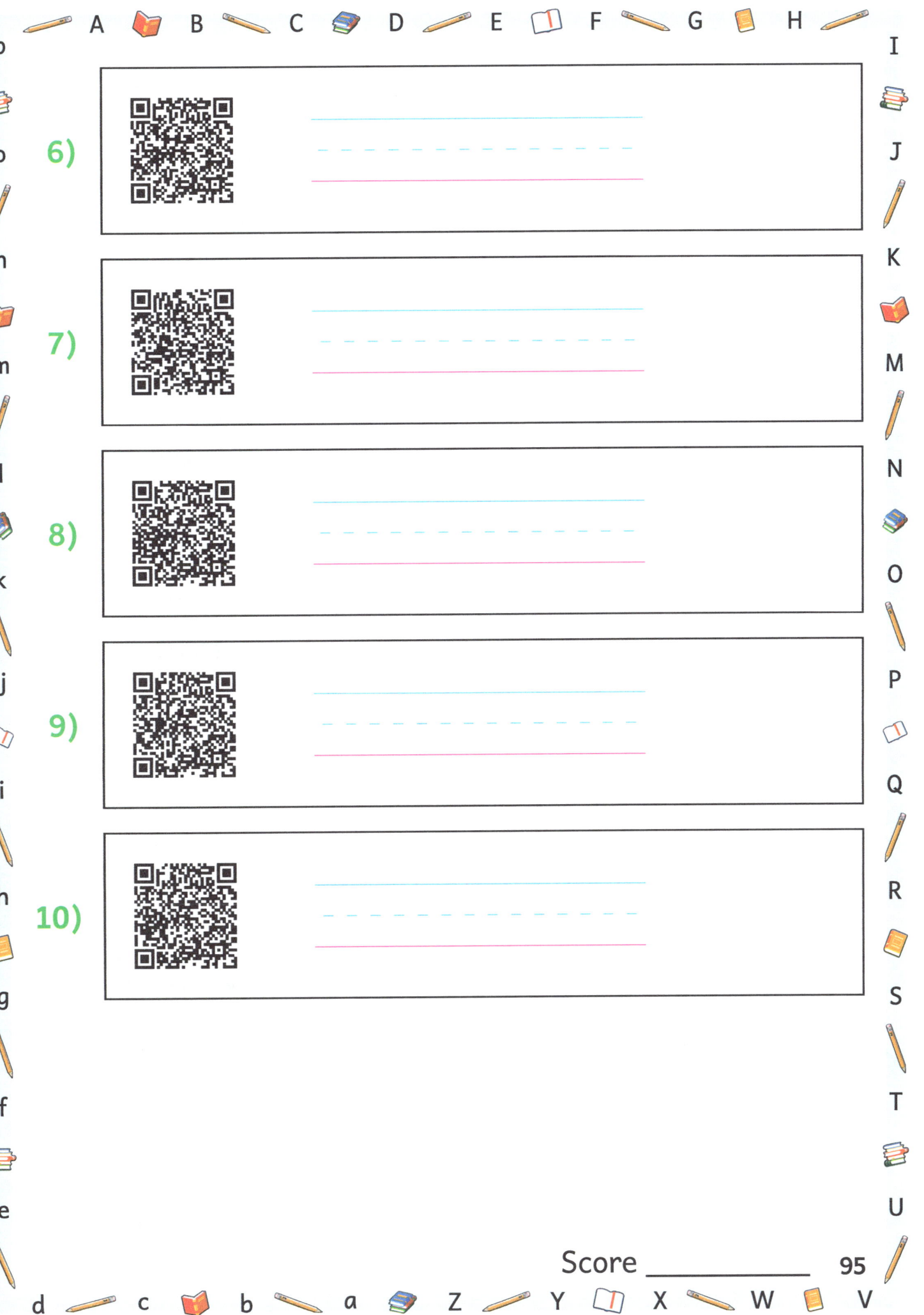

Everyday Words

 **Set a timer and read the words.**

a	the	we	I
my	by	so	go
no	try	why	made
name	like	time	home
use	white		

Time: _____

Did your time get better?